Mick & Nova's Code Busters

by

Christopher P. N. Maselli

Carson-Dellosa Publishing Company, Inc.
Greensboro, North Carolina

Credits

It is the mission of Carson-Dellosa Christian Publishing to create the highest-quality Scripture-based children's products that teach the Word of God, share His love and goodness, assist in faith development, and glorify His Son, Jesus Christ.

". . . teach me your ways so I may know you. . . ."
Exodus 33:13

For my son, Lyric. May God's Word be your code key to the mysteries of life.

Editor .... Pamela Holley-Bright
Layout Design .... Nick Greenwood
Inside Illustrations .... Nick Greenwood, Clint Moore
Cover Design................. Nick Greenwood
Cover Illustration .... Nick Greenwood

Unless otherwise marked, all Scripture is taken from the HOLY BIBLE, NEW INTERNATIONAL VERSION®. Copyright © 1973, 1978, 1984 by International Bible Society. Used by permission of Zondervan Bible Publishers.

Scripture marked NIrV is taken from the Holy Bible, NEW INTERNATIONAL READER'S VERSION®. Copyright © 1996, 1998 International Bible Society. All rights reserved throughout the world. Used by permission of International Bible Society.

ISBN: 978-1-60022-059-3

Table of Contents

Confidential Information

For Your Eyes Only!

Greetings, Super Sleuth! You're about to have a boatload of mind-bending fun! Nova and I are best friends and known to many as the Super Sleuth Investigators. You might have read some of our *Sleuth-It Yourself* mysteries:

Smarter than the Average Pair

Secret of the Firm Foundations

The Gifts from Outer Space

Invasion of the Psalm Psnatchers

Fruit Encounters of the God Kind

Attack of the Tremendous Truth

Now, you can discover how to do something every super sleuth must be able to do: create and decipher codes!

This book is jam-packed with 30 challenging codes that will teach you just how a super

sleuth thinks. Best of all, while you're cracking codes, you'll also be unlocking the mysteries of the Bible. This is super because Nova and I believe God's Word holds the solutions to all of life's mysteries. So get to it! And don't just solve each code once and move on . . . start using them with your family and friends!

The Inside Track

Mick's right—this book is fun, and it can be used in many ways. If you're a kid who wants to learn about codes and how to crack them, you're all set. You can start code-busting on page one. Since there are 30 codes, you could even do one a day like a devotional, and have the whole book finished in a month.

If you're a teacher or Sunday School instructor, you'll love that these code sheets can be easily torn out and duplicated for your class. And on the previous page, there's a list of Bible topics covered in this book—so you can easily find

one to support what you're teaching.

But the fun doesn't end there! Each code not only includes a mini-teaching, but also activities—one that is always a memory verse. And at the end of each topic, you'll find a section called "Under Investigation." This is like a personal spy journal where you can write down ways to put the biblical truth you've discovered into practice.

There's plenty of fun for everyone So get ready . . . and start code-busting!

GOD'S PROMISES

The Bible is a big book . . . and that's partly because it's *packed* with God's promises to us! In fact, the Bible is filled with more than 1,800 promises. Each one is there to help you grow strong in Him, be encouraged, and live without fear. You can trust God's promises.

Anything God says is true and full of life. And if He promised something to you, you can be sure it will come to pass (Isaiah 55:11). It's important to read the Bible and search for His promises because they are very valuable . . . they can even save your life! (Psalm 19:7–14) So don't hesitate. Crack open your Bible today and find out about all the good things God has for you!

Code Key

A	B	C	D	E	F	G	H	I	J	K	L	M	N	O	P	Q	R	S	T	U	V	W	X	Y	Z
1	2	3	4	5	6	7	8	9	10	11	12	13	14	15	16	17	18	19	20	21	22	23	24	25	26

Bust the Code: To read this code, all you have to do is match the number with the letter above it. So, A = 1, B = 2, and so on. Get it?

B	U	S	T	E	D
2	21	19	20	5	4

Secret!

This popular code may seem really simple, and it is . . . but it's important to understand it because *a lot* of codes in this book are based on it! In fact, you could come up with 400,000,000,000,000,000, 000,000,000 different combinations. And, no, we don't know what you call that number . . . other than *a lot!*

Word Cipher

Using the code key, decipher the missing words in Isaiah 55:11 and Psalm 145:13 NIrV to see what God says about His promises.

... my ____ ____ ____ ____ ... will not
      23   15   18   4

____ ____ ____ ____ ____ ____ to me
18   5   20   21   18   14

____ ____ ____ ____ ____ , but will
5   13   16   20   25

____ ____ ____ ____ ____ ____ ____ ____ ____ ____
1   3   3   15   13   16   12   9   19   8

what I ____ ____ ____ ____ ____ ____ and
       4   5   19   9   18   5

____ ____ ____ ____ ____ ____ ____ the
1   3   8   9   5   22   5

____ ____ ____ ____ ____ ____ ____ for which I sent it.
16   21   18   16   15   19   5

The ____ ____ ____ ____ is
    12   15   18   4

____ ____ ____ ____ ____ ____ ____ ____
6   1   9   20   8   6   21   12

and will ____ ____ ____ ____ all of his
         11   5   5   16

____ ____ ____ ____ ____ ____ ____ ____ .
16   18   15   13   9   19   5   19

Search-In-Code

Can you find the following five words coded in the word search below? Replace the numbers with their respective letters in the table below to successfully complete the word search.

PROMISE   GOD   TRUE   BIBLE   SEARCH

Bonus: Find MICK and NOVA!

13	9	3	11	7	1	2
5	20	6	14	15	22	1
7	18	18	9	4	10	2
11	21	12	3	17	15	9
19	5	1	18	3	8	2
16	18	13	15	15	5	12
16	18	15	13	9	19	5

Under Investigation

What is something God promises you?
How many of God's promises are sure to happen?

GOD IS LOVE

Depending on who you talk to, people have some pretty crazy ideas about who God is. Some people think He's an angry guy with a big stick, just looking for people to knock down. Other people think He's just "up there somewhere," and doesn't care much what goes on down here on earth.

But the Bible is very clear: God isn't either of those things. God is, to put it simply, love! (1 John 4:8) Everything He does stems out of His pure and intense love for us. In fact, He loves us so much that He sent His Son, Jesus, to the world, to take our place and die for our sins so that we could live (John 3:16). And He didn't do that because we did something to deserve His help . . . He just loves us!

Code Key

	1	2	3	4	5
1	A	B	C	D	E
2	F	G	H	IJ	K
3	L	M	N	O	P
4	Q	R	S	T	U
5	V	W	X	Y	Z

Bust the Code: To read this one, first you find the correct row on the left, then find the correct column on top. The letter you're looking for is where the two cross in the table. So, if you see the number 43, that means you must find where row 4 and column 3 cross. The letter at that spot is the one you want. In this case, it's "S"! Get it?

P.S. Number 24 is either "I" or "J"—you have to figure out which letter your code needs when you decipher it.

B	U	S	T	E	D
12	45	43	44	15	14

Secret!

This code, called the "Polybius Checkerboard," was created by Polybius, a Greek historian, who lived from 203 BC to 120 BC!

Word Cipher

Using the code key, decipher 1 John 4:10 NIrV to answer the question: What is love?

It is that he ___ ___ ___ ___ ___   ___ ___
               31   34   51   15   14   45   43

and sent His ___ ___ ___ to ___ ___ ___ ___
            43 34 33   22 24 51 15

His ___ ___ ___ ___ to ___ ___ ___
    31 24 21 15   35 11 54

for our ___ ___ ___ ___ .
        43 24 33 43

Joke-In-Code

Mick: Have you ever seen a man-eating shark?

Nova: Hmmm . . . no but . . .

...I once saw a ___ ___ ___ ___
                 22 24 42 31

___ ___ ___ ___ ___ ___
15 11 44 24 33 22

___ ___ ___ ___ ___ ___ ___ !
31 34 12 43 44 15 42

Under Investigation

What is one word you'd use to describe God's love?
Who can you share God's love with this week?

Code 03:

STOPPING STRIFE

God doesn't want us to fight with each other. He wants us to have peace in our homes, in our churches, and with our friends. But still, it's easy to start a quarrel with one another. We don't usually do it on purpose either . . . sometimes fighting words just slip out.

The Bible says when words slip out like that, they're like a leak in a dam (Proverbs 17:14). It may start off as "no big deal," but let it continue and you'll have a flood of trouble! So take a stand against strife today . . . and when fighting words enter your mind, stop them in their tracks. Choose to live in peace.

Code Key

1	2	3	4	5	6	7	8	9	10	11	12	13	14	15	16	17	18	19	20	21	22	23	24	25	26
A	B	C	D	E	F	G	H	I	J	K	L	M	N	O	P	Q	R	S	T	U	V	W	X	Y	Z

Bust the Code: You know this code key . . . A = 1, B = 2 and so on. But here's the twist: to get the number to decode, you have to solve a math problem first. So 4 x 1 = 4 and then, 4 = D. Get it?

B	U	S	T	E	D
2	27	10	10	10	4
+0	−6	+9	×2	−5	×1
2	21	19	20	5	4

Secret!

Believe it or not, music is highly mathematical. Rhythm, measures, keys, tuning, and more are all tied to basic math concepts. So, the next time you want to scream during a math test, just remember that the tune floating through your head couldn't have been written without it.

Word Cipher

Solving the math problems and using the code key, decipher the missing words in Proverbs 17:14 to see what God says you should do when a quarrel starts.

Starting a ____ ____ ____ ____ ____ ____ ____ is like

$$\begin{array}{ccccccc} 10 & 11 & 7 & 9 & 17 & 5 & 6 \\ +7 & +10 & -6 & \times 2 & +1 & \times 1 & \times 2 \end{array}$$

breaching a ____ ____ ____ ; so ____ ____ ____ ____

$$\begin{array}{ccccccc} 6 & 2 & 9 & & 2 & 9 & 13 & 4 \\ -2 & -1 & +4 & & \times 2 & \times 2 & +2 & +12 \end{array}$$

the ____ ____ ____ ____ ____ ____ before a dispute

$$\begin{array}{cccccc} 13 & 1 & 10 & 18 & 7 & 15 \\ \times 1 & \times 1 & \times 2 & +2 & -2 & +3 \end{array}$$

____ ____ ____ ____ ____ ____ out.

$$\begin{array}{cccccc} 1 & 11 & 4 & 21 & 11 & 22 \\ +1 & +7 & +1 & -20 & \times 1 & -3 \end{array}$$

Super-Long Math Code

Solve this super-long math code to find out: Why was the math book so mad?

$$\begin{array}{cccccccc} 8 & 1 & 15 & 2 & 13 & 0 & 2 & 141 \\ +2 & +1 & \times 1 & +1 & +3 & \times 0 & +1 & \times 33 \\ -5 & \times 2 & +5 & -2 & -10 & +4 & +2 & +3242 \\ \times 3 & \times 2 & -5 & \times 6 & \times 3 & \times 0 & +9 & -77 \\ +5 & \times 2 & -15 & -3 & -2 & \times 0 & +2 & \times 0 \\ -4 & +2 & +15 & -1 & -4 & +5 & -3 & +19 \end{array}$$

Because it had big ___ ___ ___ ___ ___ ___ ___ ___ !

Under Investigation

What happens if a dam leak isn't stopped?
What can replace strife?

Code 04:

SALVATION

Have you ever felt like you've done everything wrong and you'd just like to be able to start over? Well, here's good news: God wants to give you a brand new start. He knew we would mess up and need Him . . . that's why Jesus came to earth, lived without ever doing anything wrong, and then died—so that we wouldn't have to die for our wrongs.

Now, we can say, "Jesus, I'm giving you my life. I'm following You." And when we do, nothing will ever be the same again. When He looks at us, God doesn't see our wrongs . . . He sees Jesus' right. And that not only gives us a new start, but it gives us a new finish, too . . . for if we open up our hearts to Him, we will live forever with Him in heaven!

Code Key

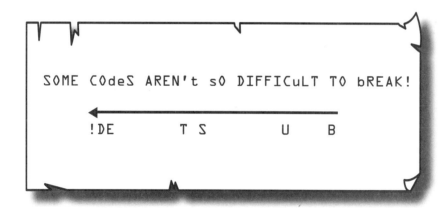

SOME COdeS AREN't sO DIFFICuLT TO bREAK!

!DE   T S   U   B

Bust the Code: This code is simple . . . just use upper-case and lower-case letters, like ABC and abc. Here's the spin—to bust the code, you only read the lower-cased letters, and you read it backward!

Secret!

Calling letters "upper case" and "lower case" started in 1588 in the printing press industry. In English, lower case is used far more than upper case, simply because most of the time we only use upper case to start sentences or signify proper nouns.

Word Cipher

Using this code, decipher the first and last portions of Romans 10:13.

CHICKenS LoVE NEW yEARrS eve

... who calls on the name of the Lord ...

deNvER CHaseD bIll iN THE wINTER SNOW.

_____

_____

_____

Opposites

Can you decode these words and figure out which words are opposites? Match the opposite words by drawing a line to connect them.

tOLEDO ohIO_____   troTTING hORsE_____

tHe wHALE_____   SALtY salT_____

puNY_____   COLd locATION_____

lONGITUDE laTItUDE_____   nOT woOdEN_____

TAtER TOTs AND riFF-RAfF_____   TWISTy rOAd_____

Under Investigation

Who can call on Jesus for help?
Have you ever given Jesus rule over your life?

GOD'S WORD

The Bible is called "God's Word" because it's a book written by God! He used people to put the words on the paper, but the promises, truths, and wisdom are all from Him. The Bible is unlike any other book. It's "living and active" and not only shows us the difference between right and wrong, but it also helps us judge our thoughts and attitudes (Hebrews 4:12). It's important to read God's Word often. It's full of wisdom for life . . . wisdom that can change and even save our lives!

Code Key

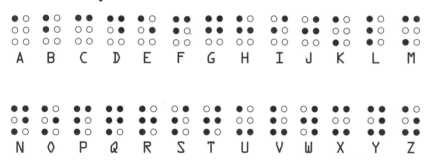

Bust the Code: This code is based on Braille. To decode it, just match the dots with the letter they represent. Get it?

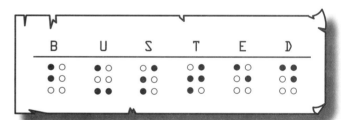

Secret!

Braille is a system that blind people use to read. It is comprised of dots in six possible positions, and in the real world, the "dots" are raised for easy reading by touch. It was developed nearly 200 years ago by Louis Braille, and actually stemmed from a system the French created to give their soldiers the ability to communicate silently at night.

Word Cipher

Using the code key, decipher the missing words in Psalm 119:105 to see how God's Word helps us.

Your ____ ____ ____ ____ is a ____ ____ ____ ____

to my ____ ____ ____ ____ and a ____ ____ ____ ____ ____

for my ____ ____ ____ ____ .

Joke-in-Code

Nova: What has a truck, a tail, and two gray ears?

Mick: That's easy!

Mick:
It's obviously a ____ ____ ____ ____ ____

____ ____ ____ ____ ____ ____ ____ ____ ____ ____ !

Under Investigation

Why should you read God's Word?
How does God's Word help you?

Code 06:

PERSECUTION

Jesus said when we follow Him, sometimes people will make fun of us, insult us, or maybe even try to hurt us. That may seem scary, but Jesus said when it happens, we should be glad! Why? Because He's got a great reward for us in heaven.

Jesus knows what He's talking about, too—people gave Him and the prophets trouble all of the time. So if someone insults you because of your faith, consider yourself standing in good company. (The best!)

Code Key

7 298683 451124

1. BUSTED
2. CAN
3. THIS
4. CODE
5. IS
6. FRIENDS
7. YOU
8. YOUR, THAT
9. TELL

Bust the Code: This code uses a number system you use almost every day: UPC symbols—you know, those funny-looking bar codes on products. To decode this barcode, use the numbered list of words below, reading them in the order of the bar code's numbers. So the first word is #7: YOU, then #2: CAN, then #9: TELL, and so on. Extra numbers can be dropped once the code is read. Get it?

You	can	tell	your	friends	that	this	code	is	busted!	-	-	-
7	2	9	8	6	8	3	4	5	1	1	2	4

Secret!

UPC symbols were first used by grocery stores in the 1970s. Since then, they've grown in great popularity as store owners use them to easily keep their inventory up-to-date. Legend says that the first UPC symbol ever scanned was on a pack of bubble gum.

Word Cipher

Using the UPC symbols below, decipher the scripture to see what Jesus said you should do when you're persecuted.

||||||| 8394 ||| 7216 ||||||

1. YOU
2. INSULT
3. ARE
4. WHEN
5. SOLVED
6. ...
7. PEOPLE
8. "BLESSED
9. YOU

|||||| 6 597281 547385 ||||||

1. REWARD
2. IS
3. 5
4. HEAVEN...."
5. GLAD, IN, -
6. BE
7. GREAT, MATTHEW
8. YOUR, 11—12
9. BECAUSE

_____
_____
_____
_____
_____
_____
_____

Funny Facts

Decode these UPC symbols to read some funny facts!

||||||| 4728 ||| 9154 ||||||

1. MILES
2. CAN
3. PICKLES
4. SOME, HOUR
5. PER
6. TRUE
7. PENGUINS
8. SWIM
9. 22

_____
_____
_____
_____
_____
_____
_____

||||||| 6235 ||| 7814 ||||||

1. PER
2. AVERAGE
3. PERSON
4. MINUTE
5. BLINKS
6. THE
7. 25
8. TIMES
9. PIZZA

_____
_____
_____
_____
_____
_____
_____

Under Investigation

What will you do when someone insults you because you follow Jesus?
When were you insulted because you chose to follow Jesus?

Code 07:

HEARING GOD'S VOICE

Did you know God is talking to you? It's true! If you listen, you can hear Him talk to your spirit. He wants to show you how to do what's right all the time (Romans 8:13–14).

But how do you know if you're hearing God's voice or not? Here's a good test to remember: God will never say anything that goes against what He has said in the Bible (John 16:13). So, as you read and get to know God's Word, you'll also become better at hearing His voice. He wants to have a conversation with you!

Code Key

A	•—	J	•———	S	•••
B	—•••	K	—•—	T	—
C	—•—•	L	•—••	U	••—
D	—••	M	——	V	•••—
E	•	N	—•	W	•——
F	••—•	O	———	X	—••—
G	——•	P	•——•	Y	—•——
H	••••	Q	——•—	Z	——••
I	••	R	•—•		

Bust the Code: This code is based on Morse code. To decode it, just match the lines and dots with the letter they represent. Get it?

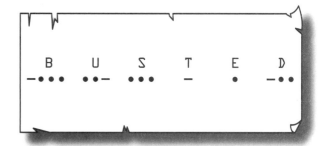

B	U	S	T	E	D
—•••	••—	•••	—	•	—••

Secret!

Morse code was created in the 1830s to send messages across Samuel Morse's electric telegraph. It can be tapped on a computer or even signaled with lights or flags as short and long bursts to match the dashes and dots. One dash is equal to the length of three dots. Many people call the dashes "dahs" and the dots "dits."

Word Cipher

Using the code key, decipher the missing words in John 10:27 and Psalm 29:4 to see a truth about hearing Jesus' voice.

My ____ ____ ____ ____ ____
   •••   ••••   •   •   •−−•

____ ____ ____ ____ ____ ____
•−•• •• ••• − • −•

to my ____ ____ ____ ____ ____ ; I
   •••− −−− •• −•−• •

____ ____ ____ ____ them, and they
−•− −• −−− •−−

____ ____ ____ ____ ____ ____ me.
••−• −−− •−•• •−•• −−− •−−

The ____ ____ ____ ____ ____ of the Lᴏʀᴅ is
  •••− −−− •• −•−• •

____ ____ ____ ____ ____ ____ ____ ____ ; the
•−−• −−− •−− • •−• ••−• ••− •−••

voice of the ____ ____ ____ ____ is majestic.
   •−•• −−− •−• −••

Under Investigation

Have you ever heard God speak to you?
What is something God might say?

Code 08:

HEART MATTERS

People sure have a lot of silly ideas about what's important. Many work their whole lives so that they can drive a flashy car, have a big house, and receive the respect of their peers. While there's nothing wrong with cars, houses, or being respected, those aren't the most important things to God. What He's really interested in is your heart. Are you listening to Jesus? Are you living for Him? Do you want to please Him more than you please anyone else? If so, God will see that . . . and others will, too.

Code Key

♥ = 1

♠ = 5

♡ = 10

⌄ = 20

Bust the Code: To bust this one, just count the grouped hearts, adding them together. Then match the resulting number with the letter in the code key above. So, a big upside down heart with a little heart and a little upside down heart inside would equal 26 (20+5+1), which equals "V." Get it?

5	6	7	8	9	10	11	12	13	14	15	16	17	18	19	20	21	22	23	24	25	26	1	2	3	4
A	B	C	D	E	F	G	H	I	J	K	L	M	N	O	P	Q	R	S	T	U	V	W	X	Y	Z

B U S T E D

Secret!

No one knows for sure how the heart symbol got its shape. Some believe it looks like a cow's heart—which in the old days was the only kind of heart most people might have seen. Others say it looks like the seed from a plant that is now extinct. Wherever it came from, the heart is almost always drawn red—symbolizing blood, emotion, and passion.

Word Cipher

Using the hearts below and the code key, decipher the missing words in 1 Samuel 16:7 to see what is important to the Lord.

"

_____ looks at the _____

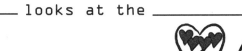 

_____, but the

_____ looks at the

_____."

Name Cluster

Using the space below, draw heart clusters that spell the letters in your name.

Under Investigation

What does God see when He looks in your heart?
How do others see Jesus in you?

ANGELS

God has special servants watching over you: Angels! You may not see them, but the Bible says angels watch over you, protect you, and help you (Hebrews 1:14). Angels are cool, but God says we shouldn't worship them. Our worship is for God and God alone. So, the next time you see trouble brewing, remember that you have angels nearby. They may even appear and look like normal people, even though you'd never know it (Hebrews 13:2). God thinks of everything, doesn't He?

Code Key

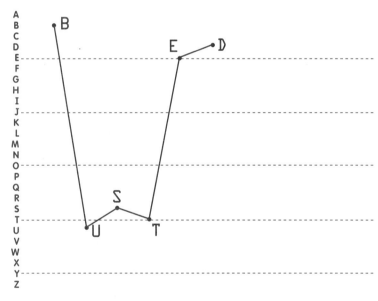

Bust the Code: This code looks like a big line chart, like businesses use to show that their sales are rising or falling. But it's really a secret message! To bust this one, just read left to right. Every time you see a dot, it represents the letter directly across from it. Get it?

B U S T E D

Secret!

Graphs are used today for a variety of reasons, usually to provide information. In this way, graphs are a "visual language" similar to maps or drawings.

CD-204049 *Mick and Nova's Code Busters*

Word Cipher

Using the line graph below, decipher the last part of Psalm 91:11 to see how angels help you.

```
For he will command his angels concerning you to . . .
```

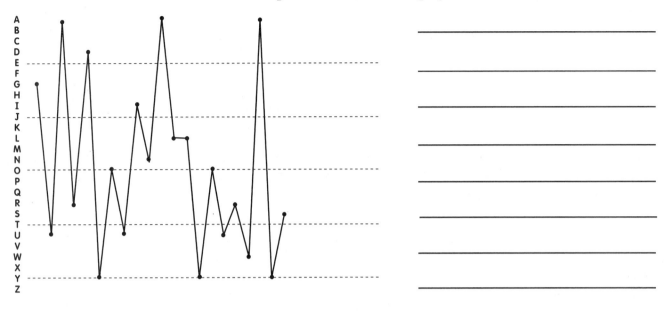

_____

_____

_____

_____

_____

_____

_____

Graph It

Graph the names of everyone in your house that you know angels are protecting.

_____

_____

_____

_____

_____

_____

_____

Under Investigation

What is something angels do for you?
When is a time you know angels helped you?

Code 10:

LAUGHTER

In a world where people always find reasons to be sad, God says He wants us to live lives of joy! The apostle Paul encouraged us to rejoice in the Lord all the time. In other words, when things try to get you down, smile! Joy in God brings strength (Nehemiah 8:10), just when you need it most. And when others see how happy you are, they'll see Jesus in you and it will bless them. So go ahead and laugh out loud . . . it'll do you good!

Code Key

1	2	3	4	5	6	7	8	9	10	11	12	13	14	15	16	17	18	19	20	21	22	23	24	25	26
A	B	C	D	E	F	G	H	I	J	K	L	M	N	O	P	Q	R	S	T	U	V	W	X	Y	Z

Bust the Code: You know this code key . . . A = 1, B = 2 and so on. But here's the twist: to get the number to decode, you have to add the five numbers in the 5-digit "zip code" first. So for the zip code 53510, 5 + 3 + 5 + 1 + 0 = 14 and then 14 = N. Get it?

B	U	S	T	E	D
10001	71931	22276	48332	21101	12010

Secret!

Zip codes started in 1943, to help mail get to the right place quickly. Here's what the five numbers stand for in a real zip code, such as 51106:

1st number = the national service area

2nd number = the subdivision of the national service area

3rd number = the city

4th and 5th numbers = the post office station in the city

Word Cipher

Using the zip codes below and the code key, decipher the missing words in Proverbs 17:22 to see what the Bible says about laughter.

A ‾‾‾‾‾ ‾‾‾‾‾ ‾‾‾‾‾ ‾‾‾‾‾ ‾‾‾‾‾ ‾‾‾‾‾ ‾‾‾‾‾ ‾‾‾‾‾
  20010   32111   21011   11111   74142   30003   92442   53211

‾‾‾‾‾ ‾‾‾‾‾ ‾‾‾‾‾ ‾‾‾‾‾ ‾‾‾‾‾ is good
11420   01040   00100   83241   93620

‾‾‾‾‾ ‾‾‾‾‾ ‾‾‾‾‾ ‾‾‾‾‾ ‾‾‾‾‾ ‾‾‾‾‾ ‾‾‾‾‾ ‾‾‾‾‾. . . .
63103   30200   01111   34200   01020   20304   70151   20102

Knock-Knock!

Read this knock-knock by completing the code.

Mick: Knock, knock!

Nova: Who's there?

Mick: ‾‾‾‾‾ ‾‾‾‾‾ ‾‾‾‾‾ ‾‾‾‾‾ ‾‾‾‾‾!
     73122 44220 10224 90139 21011

Nova: ‾‾‾‾‾ ‾‾‾‾‾ ‾‾‾‾‾ ‾‾‾‾‾ ‾‾‾‾‾ who?
     44430 12342 00009 71707 11111

Mick: ‾‾‾‾‾ ‾‾‾‾‾ ‾‾‾‾‾ ‾‾‾‾‾ ‾‾‾‾‾ to
     35232 33303 33300 87502 41000

‾‾‾‾‾ ‾‾‾‾‾ ‾‾‾‾‾ ‾‾‾‾‾ ‾‾‾‾‾ codes!
63321 54321 24321 97321 21020

Under Investigation

What will you do next time trouble comes?
What does joy give you?

MISSION: POSSIBLE

What seems impossible to you? What is something in your life that is such a mess that you can't even dream of how it can be fixed? Whatever it is, God has a message for you: With Him, anything is possible (Mark 9:23).

Think of the stories in the Bible. Jesus had to feed 5,000 people with five loaves of bread and two fish. Seem impossible? Not to God. Little David had to defeat a giant with nothing but a small rock. Seem impossible? Not to God. So what is that thing that seems impossible in your life? It's not impossible to God! He can do more than we could ever ask or imagine (Ephesians 3:20).

Code Key

```
$u_flag = FALSE ;
    $u_type = 'B' ;
    $x_tmp = substr( $x_t,0,1 ) ;
    if ( $x_tmp=='U' )
        {
        $u_nyp = TRUE ;
        $x_u = str_repl( 'S','T',$x_t ) ;
        if ( $x_u != 'ED' )
            {
            $gk = str_repl( $x_u,'',$gz ) ;
            }
```

Bust the Code: This one is much easier than it looks. What looks like a computer language is really a carefully created code. To decipher it, all you have to do is ONLY read the letters between the single quotes. Get it?

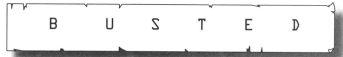

B U S T E D

Secret!

Computer code isn't really in code at all. It's just a list of instructions for a computer to obey. Nonetheless, if you're not familiar with how to read it, it sure looks like it's in code!

Word Cipher

Search through this code to find Luke 18:27—a scripture verse about what God can do.

```
$ba = FALSE ;
    $x = strpos( $gk,'whA'! ) ;
    if ( is_integer($x) )
        if ( $x == 0 )
            {
            $y2 = $ar['TiS'] ;
            if ( $y2 == '' ):
                    $ba = TRUE ;
            else:
                    $t = $y2 ;
            endif;
            $li = strlen( 'imp'$gk 'oss' $li 'Ibl''e' ) - 1 ;
            $gk'w' = substr( $gk,'ithm',$li, 'en' ) ;
            }
        if ( $x > 0 )
            {
            $t = $ar['isp'] ;
            $gk = str_replace( 'oss','Ibl',$gk, 'e' ) ;
            }
        $x = strpos( $gk,'with' ) ;
    if ( is_integer($x) )
        {
        $t = $t . $ar['GO'] ;
        $gk = str_replace( 'd','',$gk ) ;
        }
 $x = strpos( $gk,'' ) ;
    endif ;
```

Re: Draw

Rewrite these characters in the proper row order (or cut out the rows and reorder them) to reveal something "impossible" that God did!

5	@| @@@@@	|	\	|	\	|		|	\ |		
3	@ -- @@@	|	|	|	|	|		|\	|	8	
1	He is ...										
4	@| @@@@@	|--	|	\	|--	|	\	|	8		
6	@ -- @@@	|	|	|	---	--	|		|	8	
2	@@@@@	--	|	--	--	|		|	8		

1	
2	.
3	
4	
5	
6	

Under Investigation

What impossible thing do you believe God will do for you?
When was a time God did something impossible for you?

Code 12:

COURAGE

At one time or another, we all face something scary. But God has one word for us: courage! God says we don't have to be afraid of what may come or what others think . . . because He is our refuge and strength. He is an ever-present help in trouble (Psalm 46:1). So, what do we have to be afraid of? The next time you face a scary situation, remember: God is with you. Have courage! He won't let you down.

Code Key

1	2 ABC	3 DEF
4 GHI	5 JKL	6 MNO
7 PQRS	8 TUV	9 WXYZ
*	0	#

Bust the Code: Look familiar? It's a telephone keypad. To bust the code, you'll be given sets of double-digit numbers. The first number in each set tells you which box to start in. The second tells you which letter in the box to use. So, for instance, the number 93 tells you to go to the ninth box and use the third letter: "Y." Get it?

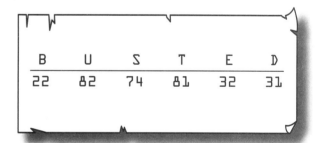

B U S T E D
22 82 74 81 32 31

Secret!

While the number and letter layout shown above is now the international standard, it hasn't always been that way. Until recently, most phones in the U.S. left out the "O," "Q" and "Z" completely.

Word Cipher

Using the code key, decipher the missing words in Joshua 1:9 to see why God says you can have courage.

"Be _____ _____ _____ _____ _____ _____ and
    74   81   73   63   62   41

_____ _____ _____ _____ _____ _____ _____ _____ _____ _____
23   63   82   73   21   41   32   63   82   74

. . . for the _____ _____ _____ _____ your
             53   63   73   31

_____ _____ _____ will be _____ _____ _____ _____
41   63   31   91   43   81   42

_____ _____ _____ wherever you go."
93   63   82

Square-Teaser

Here's a quick brain-teaser. How many perfect squares are on this number pad? Don't answer too fast! There are more than you think . . .

There are _____ squares.

1	2 ABC	3 DEF
4 GHI	5 JKL	6 MNO
7 PQRS	8 TUV	9 WXYZ
*	0	#

Under Investigation

Why does God want you to have courage?
When was a time you had courage?

WHO TO SERVE?

There are a lot of things competing for our attention. But sooner or later, we make the decision to give our time, our thoughts, and our energy to one thing above all. God hopes we'll choose to serve Him above all else. That's why He challenges us, asking, "Who will you serve?" (Joshua 24:15)

Some people serve money. Others spend their days serving sports, others—video games, others—their friends. But Jesus said we can't serve two masters at once (Matthew 6:24). We have to decide who's number one in our lives. What will your choice be?

Code Key

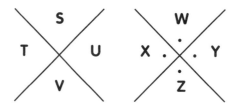

Bust the Code: To break this code, find where the symbol sits in the code key above—then use the letter in its place. Get it?

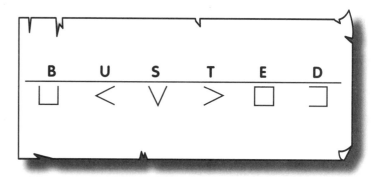

B	U	S	T	E	D
⊔	<	∨	>	□	⊐

Secret!

This code is commonly called the Pigpen Cipher because the grids resemble animal pens. It has been around for hundreds of years and some believe it originated with a group that clashed with Christians. Over time though, it has become just another fun code to learn about. Many people think it looks like alien writing.

Word Cipher

Using the code key, decipher the missing words in Joshua 24:15 to see who we should serve.

"But as for _____ and my _____,
       ·□   □·<∨□□·□

we will _____ the _____."
      ∨□·∧□   ·□·□

Joke-In-Code

Mick: This coded message looks like it was written by a pig!

Nova: How can you tell?

Mick: It's written with _____
       □·∧□∨□□·□

_____!
·□·□

Under Investigation

What things do some people serve?
Who will you serve?

Code 14:

TROUBLE

Wouldn't it be nice if, when you became a Christian, all of your troubles went away? Wouldn't it be nice if you never ran into trouble again? Yes, that would be great . . . but it's just not going to happen. Trouble is out there and sooner or later, each of us runs into it. Even Jesus ran into His fair share of trouble.

But don't let that get you down! When trouble comes your way, you're not left hopeless. You have a secret weapon: The Lord is on your side! You have overcome trouble because God in you is greater than any trouble the devil can toss your way (1 John 4:4).

Code Key

A B C D E F G H I J K L M N O P Q R S T U V W X Y Z

Bust the Code: This code involves the alphabet and a little counting. Here's how it works: change the first letter to the first letter after the letter listed. Change the second letter to the second letter after the letter listed. The third letter becomes the third letter after the letter listed and so on. When you reach Z, you wrap back around to A. Get it?

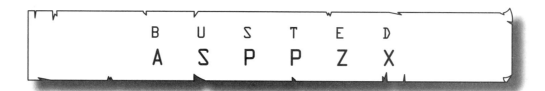

B	U	S	T	E	D
A	S	P	P	Z	X

Secret!

Ever wonder where the word "alphabet" came from? It's a combination of the Greek letters alpha and beta—the first two letters of the Greek alphabet. Alphabets come in many shapes and sizes. While many look like the letters we're used to, others aren't even printed letters . . . such as Braille, the alphabet for the blind, made with raised dots.

Word Cipher

Using the code key, decipher the missing words in Psalm 34:19 to see what the Bible says about trouble.

A righteous _____ may have _____ _____,
             LYK   LYKU   SPLQWFXK

but the_____ _____ him from
         KMOZ   CCIEQYKK

_____ _____. (Psalm 34:19)
   SFBI   ZJI

Big Trouble

Now that you understand how this brain-teasing code works, here's a trivia challenge.
If the alphabet were one word, how would it be deciphered using this code?

A B C D E F G H I J K L M N O P Q R S T U V W X Y Z is now:

_____

Hint: There's a pattern . . .

_____

_____

Under Investigation

What trouble could God deliver you from?
When has God delivered you from trouble?

MEETING YOUR NEEDS

God is in the business of taking care of His children. He promises to meet all of your needs. What are some things you need—really need—right now? Whatever they are, God can supply those things. He has more than enough stored up for you and your family (Philippians 4:19).

"Yeah," you may think, "but I really need something BIG!" Well, good news! God is also in the business of making BIG things happen. In fact, He can do "immeasurably·more than we could ask or imagine." (Ephesians 3:20) So. . . how much can you imagine? God can do more than that!

Code Key

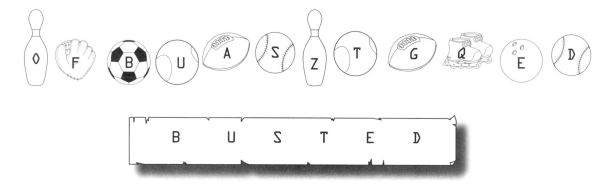

Bust the Code: Batter up! This code is packed with sports symbols. All you have to remember is to only read the sports symbols which are round balls. Nothing else counts! Get it?

Secret!

Professional baseball began in America in 1865, but many believe it is much older than that. There's a book from 1744 which has a picture of boys playing baseball in it, and a letter written in 1748 mentions how the Prince of Wales loved playing baseball.

Word Cipher

Looking only for letters in round sports balls, decipher the missing words to see Philippians 4:19.

My God will  all your

 according to his

glorious 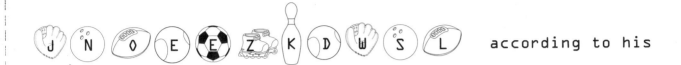 in Christ Jesus.

Maze Run

Run the football through this maze of football players from start to finish. Then, solve the code at the bottom of the page!

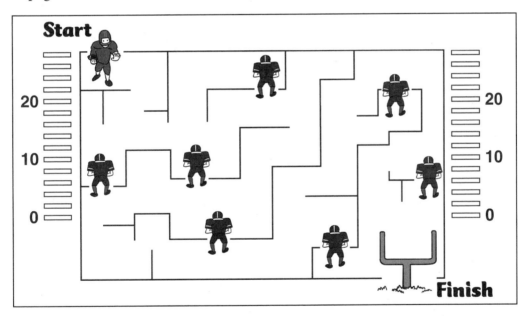

YOU HAVE MADE A .

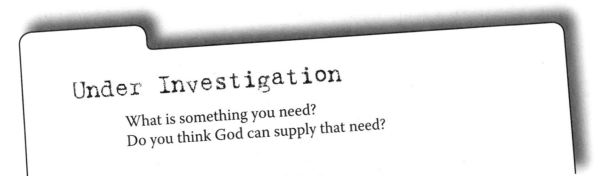

Under Investigation

What is something you need?
Do you think God can supply that need?

JESUS IS RETURNING

After Jesus rose from the dead, He went to heaven. But He's going to come back to earth! No one knows exactly when it'll happen—and many people won't be expecting it (Matthew 24:36–51). But we can be ready for Him, all prepared to say, "Welcome back! We've been expecting You!"

How do we get ready for Jesus' return? Well, of course, it's important that we keep our focus on God over anything else, and that we strive to live in a way that honors Him. Most importantly, we need to let others know about Jesus so that they can make Him their Lord, too (Luke 10:2). There's not much time left—let everyone know: Jesus is coming soon!

Code Key

Bust the Code: Some of the words in these activities have been through the shredder! To decode them, just rearrange the words in the proper order. Sound simple enough? It is until you realize that each shredded word contains one letter that doesn't belong! Get it?

BUSTED
STUMBED

Secret!

Paper shredders are created for security, so that people can shred papers with personal information on them. Today, many shredders can rip apart CDs, DVDs, and credit cards, too. For outside the home, shredders exist for shredding wood and leaves. Even the garbage disposal in your kitchen sink is a shredder (for food). But be careful! All shredders are created to cause extreme damage. . . and they can be very dangerous. So never use a shredder unless an adult is helping.

 CD-204049 *Mick and Nova's Code Busters*

Word Cipher

Unscrambling the words and throwing out the extra letters, decipher the missing words in 1 Thessalonians 5:2 to see what the Bible says about Jesus' return.

... the _____ of the _____ will _____ like

| YADA | | ROLED | | COMBE |

a _____ in the _____ .

| FIFTHE | | GEHINT |

Completely Shredded

Column by column, drop the strips into the puzzle below in the correct order to find out what Mick said to Nova after he accidentally put his report card into a shredder.

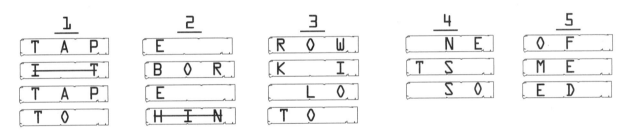

Under Investigation

When do you think Jesus will return?
What are you doing to prepare for Jesus' return?

ON THE LOOKOUT

God is on the lookout. He's looking for you. He wants to bless you and strengthen you (2 Chronicles 16:9). He wants to move in your life and in the lives of those around you. Isn't that amazing?!

Every day, He's searching for young people who will love Him with their whole hearts. How about you? What will He see when He finds you? Hopefully, He will see someone who is ready to receive Him . . . and reach out to others with love.

Code Key

$$+ \ 10 \ - \ N \ + \ D$$

Bust the Code: Anything goes! This code is fun to read as well as write! Read not only the letters, but also the pictures to figure out the code. Get it?

BUSTED
BUS + TEN − N + D

Secret!

Reading through pictures is as old as history. For ages, people have told stories through pictures called hieroglyphics, similar to those used in these codes. The Egyptians claim ownership to some of the oldest hieroglyphics found—on pottery dating back to 4000 BC—which was around the time Moses lived.

Word Cipher

Using the pictures and clues below, decipher 2 Chronicles 16:9 to see who God is looking for.

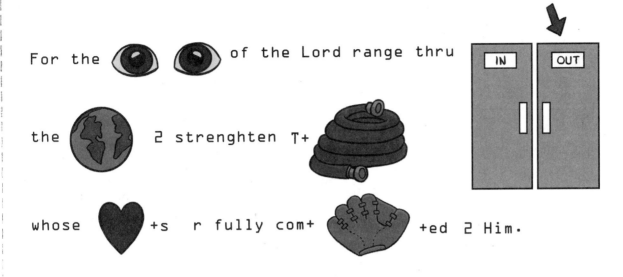

For the 👁👁 of the Lord range thru

the 🌍 2 strenghten T+ 🪢

whose ❤️+s r fully com+ 🧤 +ed 2 Him.

_____

_____

Your Turn!

Nova asked Mick to investigate a mystery at her house . . . but it was really a surprise party! Using pictures and clues, write a few sentences about what Mick saw when he opened the door.

_____

_____

_____

Under Investigation

Why is God looking for you?
What will God see when He finds you?

Code 18:

EVERYTHING CHANGES

Something amazing happened when you made Jesus the Lord of your life . . . everything in your life changed! Sure, you may look the same on the outside, but on the inside, everything is different. Your spirit—the real you—was dead and is now alive in Jesus! Any bad things you've done and all your failures are now wiped away. You get a brand new start!

Sure, you may still struggle with some things, but now you have God's power inside you. That's a big advantage. The devil can't keep a hold on you any longer. You've been set free!

Code Key

```
8U5t3d!
BUSTED
```

Bust the Code: This code uses regular letters and numbers . . . but in a very unusual way. The key to busting this code is to read it the way it sounds and the way it looks. For instance, "ne1" would be "anyone" and "VVOVV" would be "wow." Get it?

Secret!

Believe it or not, this is a real language some people use on the Internet. It's called "L33t" (short for "elite"). It began in the early 90s by computer gamers who wanted to identify themselves as hackers. Since then, because it takes so much time to type and decipher, it's fallen out of use by most Internet users. Besides, many people find it downright annoying.

Word Cipher

See if you can decipher the L33t (elite) words in 2 Corinthians 5:17 to see what the Bible says about the changes you've experienced in your life since becoming a Christian.

If ne1 is in <|-|r15t, he is a |\|3VV <r34t10|\|; the 01d has GO|\|3, the |\|3VV has <ON\3!

_____

_____

Word-in-Words

Mick and Nova found 25 words using the letters from the word

CREATION

Can you find more?

_____   _____   _____

_____   _____   _____

_____   _____   _____

_____   _____   _____

_____   _____   _____

_____   _____   _____

_____   _____   _____

_____   _____   _____

Under Investigation

What is something old that is gone now that you follow Jesus?
What is something new that you've discovered now that you follow Jesus?

Code 19:

GOD DOES NOT CHANGE

There are a lot of uncertain things in the world which can make life pretty stressful. But in the middle of all that "change" out there, here's something that God has reassured us about: He does not change (Malachi 3:6). From the beginning of time to the end, you can count on Him to be exactly who the Bible says He is: A God who loves you and wants the best for you. That's also good news because it means that when you look up a promise in the Bible, even though it was written thousands of years ago, it still holds true. God and His promises to you have not changed!

Code Key

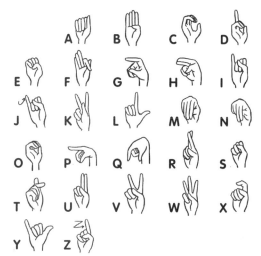

Bust the Code: This code is based on the alphabet in sign language. To decode it, just match the hand gesture with the letter. Get it?

Secret!

Some people call sign language a "universal language," thinking it's the same everywhere, but it's not! Just as there are many different spoken languages, sign language differs all over the world. It was created so that the deaf could speak just as clearly as those who use verbal words.

Word Cipher

Using the code key, decipher the missing words in Hebrews 13:8 to see a truth about Jesus.

Jesus Christ is the same _____ and

_____ and _____ .

That's a Match

Look through the sign-language letters below and find the six letters that have a match. Then unscramble those letters to uncover a secret word!

Secret word: _____

Under Investigation

Why are you glad God doesn't change?
What is one thing God has promised you?

Code 20:

DON'T GIVE UP

Have you ever been tempted to give up? Maybe when studying for a test that seemed way too hard? Or on a friend who keeps doing you wrong? Or on praying for someone who is sick? Well, don't give up!

You know God's promises are true. What He has promised you will happen. Sometimes it just takes time to "make it through." The devil wants nothing more than for you to give up. He's hoping you give up right before you see your miracle . . . whether it's understanding that subject, having your friend turn around, or seeing a loved one recover. But you have faith! You don't have to give up—you can *stand*.

Code Key

Bust the Code: Time to unlock a new code! This code is made of keys. All you have to remember is to only read the keys which point right. Nothing else counts. Get it?

B U S T E D

Secret!

You've probably heard of skeleton keys—keys which can open any kind of lock. While some companies, like automobile manufacturers, create skeleton keys for their mechanics which can open any of their cars, there's no such thing as a "true" skeleton key that can open any lock anywhere.

Word Cipher

Looking only for keys pointing to the right, decipher the missing words in Ephesians 6:13–14 to see what the Bible says about giving up.

... M I S C T K A N D _____ your,

G C R O O U N E D Y S _____, and after

you have D D O N N E _____

X E V G E Z R Y T F H I Y N G ... _____

TO STAND. H S T I H A N J D M _____

F M I W A R M . . . . _____

Under Investigation

What are you standing for?
Why is it important not to give up?

PRAISE GOD

Acts 16:23–26 tells the story of when Paul and Silas were bound and thrown in jail for telling people about Jesus. Locked up tight, did they complain or worry about what would happen next? No! They sang praises to God so loud that others heard them. Suddenly, God sent an earthquake, their bonds fell off, and the jail doors opened! There is a lot of power in praising God. Everyone should give God praise, for He deserves it (Psalm 150:6). Not only will praising God spark miracles, but it will bring you closer to Him!

Code Key

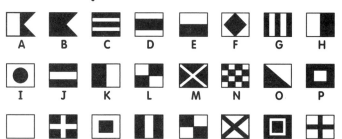

Bust the Code: This code is based on the alphabet in maritime signal flags. To decode it, just match each flag with its letter. Get it?

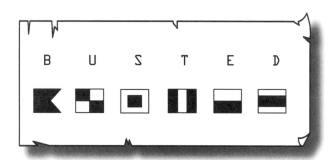

B U S T E D

Secret!

These international maritime signal flags help ships all around the world to communicate. In addition to representing letters, each flag also signals something. For instance, the "U" flag by itself also says, "You are heading for danger."

Word Cipher

Using the international maritime signal flags, decipher the missing words in Psalm 33:1 and Psalm 146:2 to see how we should praise God.

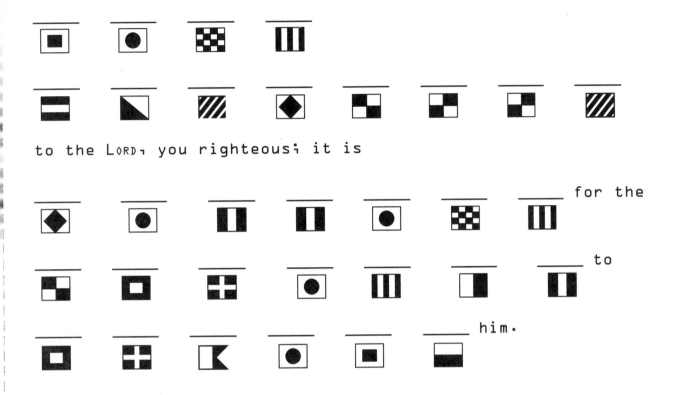

to the LORD, you righteous; it is

_____ for the

_____ to

_____ him.

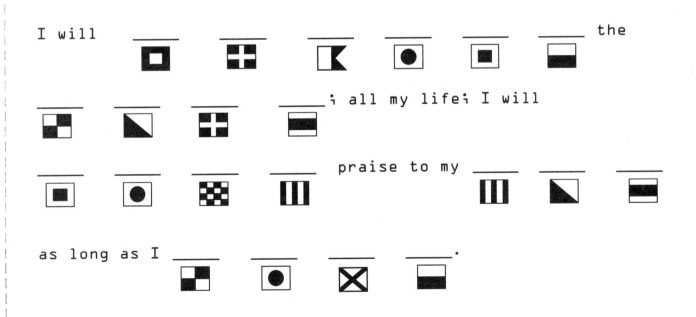

I will _____ the

_____; all my life; I will

praise to my _____ _____ _____

as long as I _____ _____ _____ _____.

Flag Scramble

Unscramble each row of flags to see the many ways you can praise God.

1.

   _ _ _ _ _ _ _ _ _ _ _ _ _____

2.

   _ _ _ _ _ _____

3.

   _ _ _ _ _____

4.

   _ _ _ _ _____

5.

   _ _ _ _ _____

6.

   _ _ _ _ _____

7.

   _ _ _ _ _ _ _ _ _ _____

   _ _ _ _ _

Under Investigation

What is one way to give God praise?
When should you praise God?

Code 22:

FORGIVE AND FORGET

Have you ever heard anyone say, "I'll forgive you, but I won't forget what you did!" Well, according to the Bible, that's not true forgiveness at all. True forgiveness is forgiving like God does . . . and the Bible says He hasn't just covered over the wrongs we've done—He's wiped them out! (Isaiah 43:25). He has forgiven us completely for *everything* . . . and we should forgive others just the same.

How many times should you forgive someone? Jesus said we should forgive as many times as it takes (Matthew 18:21–22). It may seem hard to forgive someone when they've done you wrong, but take hold of God's love and let it work through you. It will give you the strength you need to forgive that person once and for all (1 Corinthians 13:5).

Code Key

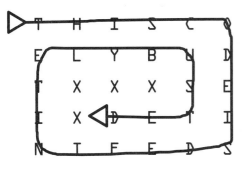

Bust the Code: This one looks like a big square of random letters . . . but really, it's a code! To read this code, start in the upper left square and read clockwise—spiraling inward until there's no more to read. If there are any boxes left over in the center, they'll be filled with X's. Get it?

This code is definitely BUSTED!

Secret!

Spirals show up in sports quite often, such as in the dance of a figure skater—or even football, where a well-thrown football spirals forward.

Word Cipher

Reading clockwise and spiraling inward, decipher the last part of Ephesians 4:32 and Colossians 3:13.

Be kind and compassionate to one another . . .

```
F   O   R   G   I   V   I
S   I   N   C   H   R   N
A   A   V   E   Y   I   G
T   G   X   X   O   S   E
S   R   X   X   U   T   A
U   O   F   D   O   G   C
J   R   E   H   T   O   H
```

_____

_____

_____

Bear with each other and forgive whatever grievances you may . . .

```
H   A   V   E   A   G   A
R   G   I   V   E   A   I
O   R   G   A   V   S   N
F   O   X   X   E   T   S
R   F   U   O   Y   H   T
E   D   R   O   L   E   O
H   T   O   N   A   E   N
```

_____

_____

_____

Super Spiral

Take this code to the next level. See if you can decipher this super spiral!

```
T   H   I   S   S   U   P   E   R   S   P   I   R
O   U   T   F   O   R   G   I   V   E   N   E   A
B   F   Y   O   U   H   O   L   D   A   N   S   L
A   I   V   E   H   I   M   S   O   T   Y   S   C
E   G   I   V   E   N   M   A   Y   H   T   M   O
S   N   G   A   U   R   S   I   F   A   H   A   D
R   I   R   E   O   X   X   N   O   T   I   R   E
E   Y   O   H   Y   X   X   S   R   Y   N   K   R
V   A   F   N   U   X   X   X   G   O   G   1   E
E   R   E   I   O   Y   E   V   I   U   A   1   V
R   P   N   R   E   H   T   A   F   R   G   2   E
U   D   O   Y   N   A   T   S   N   I   A   5   A
T   N   A   T   S   U   O   Y   N   E   H   W   L
P   I   R   C   S   R   E   H   T   O   N   A   S
```

_____

_____

_____

_____

Under Investigation

Why does God want you to forgive others?
Who is someone you need to forgive?

NO WORRIES

People worry about a lot of things. Some people worry about how to dress. Some people worry about having enough money. Others worry about what people think about them.

But are those things worth worrying about? After all, if God takes care of little things like flowers and birds, He is surely going to take care of us. He loves us so much more! (Matthew 6:25–34) So don't worry about all the things in life that beg for your attention. Instead, focus on Jesus. He is able to give us everything we need . . . and more!

Code Key

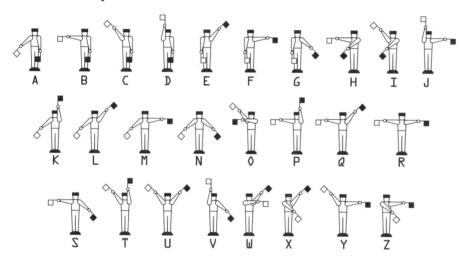

Bust the Code: This code is based on the flag semaphore system. To decode it, just match each flag signal with the letter it represents. Get it?

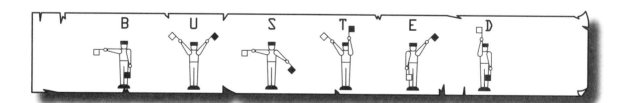

Secret!

The flag semaphore system is a way people can communicate over a short distance. It's used both on land and at sea to quickly send messages by changing the positions of hand-held flags. When used on land, red and white flags are used. When used at sea, red and yellow flags are used.

Word Cipher

Using the semaphore flag system, decipher the missing words in Matthew 6:33 to see how to receive God's blessings.

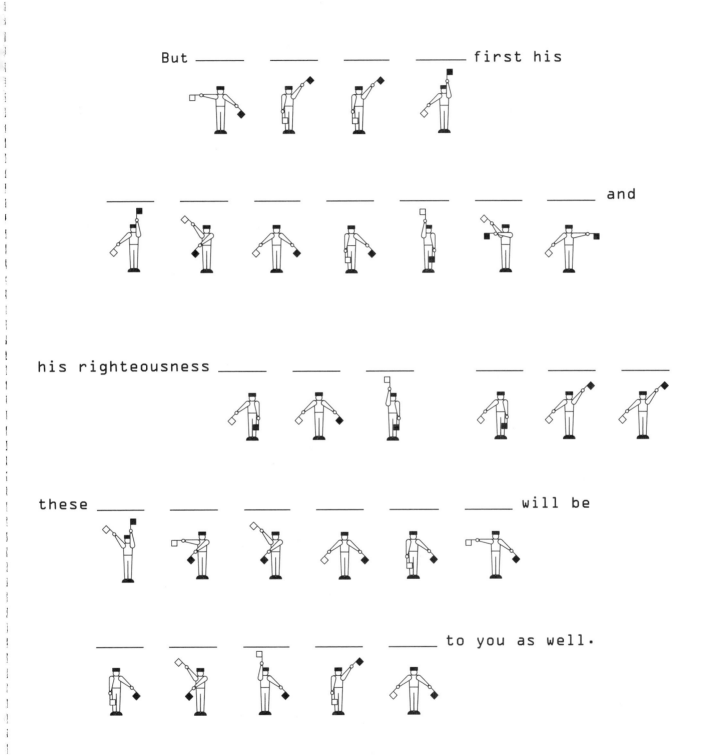

But _____ _____ _____ _____ first his

_____ _____ _____ _____ _____ _____ _____ and

his righteousness _____ _____ _____ _____ _____ _____

these _____ _____ _____ _____ _____ _____ will be

_____ _____ _____ _____ _____ to you as well.

Capture the Flag

Run through this maze from start to finish (A to Z)—moving from one adjacent flag to another in any direction . . . but be sure to stay in alphabetical order!

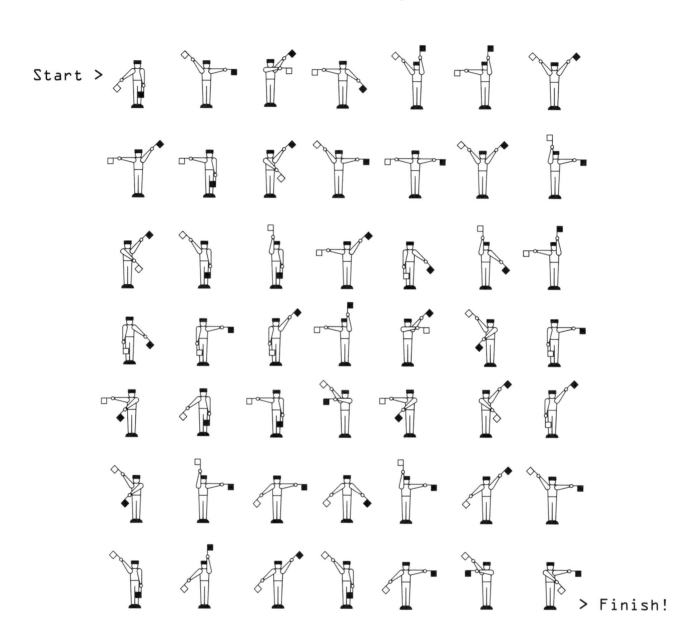

Start >

> Finish!

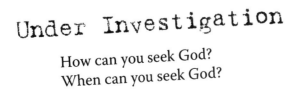

Under Investigation

How can you seek God?
When can you seek God?

Code 24:

REPRESENTING JESUS

Jesus said we are the light of the world (Matthew 5:14). And He doesn't want us to hide! He wants everyone to see our light so that they can see Jesus in us and be drawn to Him. He wants us to shine brightly, unashamed, with love and wisdom. Then when others see us, they will want to know more about Jesus. We represent Him to the world (2 Corinthians 5:20).

Do others see Jesus when they look at you? Do they hear Him when you speak? They should—because He's the Lord of your life . . . and you are the light of the world.

Code Key

Bust the Code: Recognize this code key? It's a common computer keyboard. To decode it, first match the shaded boxes with the letters on the keyboard. Then unscramble them. Get it?

Secret!

This keyboard layout is called the QWERTY layout—because the first six letters across spell "QWERTY." When people first started typing, they could type so fast that the machines couldn't keep up with them—the typebars that pressed the letters on the paper would get stuck together. To make it harder to type super-fast, the QWERTY layout was created. In today's computer age, typing super-fast is no longer a problem, but people have become so used to the QWERTY layout that we haven't switched to anything faster.

Word Cipher

Using the code key, decipher and unscramble the missing words in Matthew 5:16 to see why we should be good examples of Jesus.

... let your

before men, that they may

see your good deeds and

your

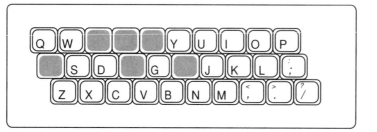

in heaven.

Memory Challenge

See how many of the letters on the keyboard you can fill in from memory.

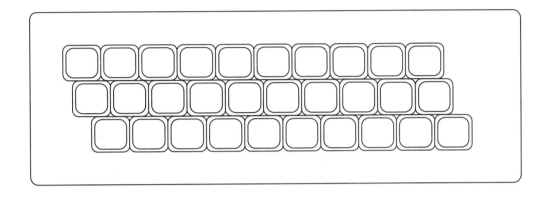

Under Investigation

What is one way others see Jesus in you?
What do others see when they look at you?

Code 25:

PEACE

Mark 4:35–41 tells the story of when Jesus was on a boat with His disciples and a powerful storm suddenly rolled in. Waves crashed over the boat and everyone thought they were going to die. Meanwhile, Jesus was fast asleep. How could Jesus possibly sleep when things seemed out of control? Because He knew He could trust God to protect Him and give Him peace. When the disciples woke Him, Jesus stood up and told the waves and the wind, "Quiet! Be still!" and they were. When things seem out of control in our lives, Jesus wants us to put our trust in Him. He can tell those problems, "Quiet! Be still!" and they will be. So don't be anxious about anything. Trust God. He will give you peace (Philippians 4:6–7).

Code Key

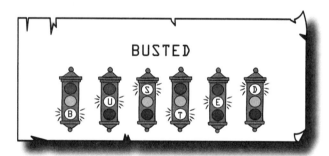

Bust the Code: Proceed with caution! This code has one stoplight after another. To decipher it, you must read the stoplights in this order: green, then yellow, then red. Then green, then yellow, then red and so on. Skip any stoplights out of that order. Get it?

Secret!

The first stoplight was created in England in 1868. It featured red and green lamps that burned gas. Less than a month after installation, it exploded. Today's electric stoplight was invented by an American, Lester Wire, in 1912, and is quite a bit safer, as it doesn't usually explode!

Word Cipher

Reading the stoplights in order below, decipher the missing words in Philippians 4:7 to see what the Bible says about peace.

And the _____ of God,

which _____

all understanding, will _____

your _____ and your

_____ in Christ

_____ .

The Right Road

Only one of these cars made it through the green light. Follow the winding streets to figure out which one!

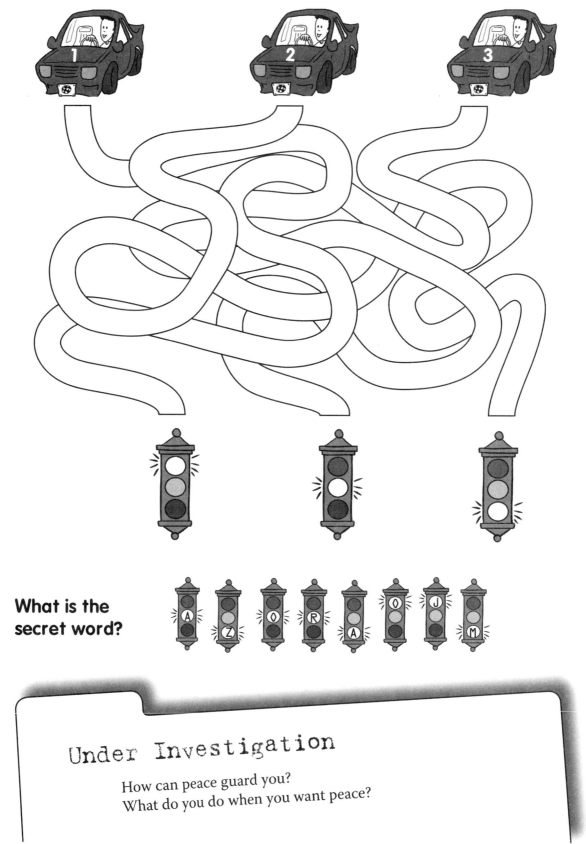

What is the secret word?

A Z O R A O J M

60

Under Investigation

How can peace guard you?
What do you do when you want peace?

WILLING AND OBEDIENT

God wants us to obey what He says. He doesn't ask us to do things because He's out to make our lives hard. He asks us to do things because they are for our good. That's why He wants us to obey. But did you know He hopes we'll do more than just obey? He wants us to be willing, too. In other words, He desires that we obey because we *want* to obey . . . not just because "He said so." When we obey God like that, the Bible says He'll have great things in store for us (Isaiah 1:19). So be obedient *and* willing!

Code Key

A	B	C	D	E	F	G	H	I	J	K	L	M
N	O	P	Q	R	S	T	U	V	W	X	Y	Z

Bust the Code: This code key takes the alphabet, cuts it in half and is solved when you realize that the letters mirror each other. So, A = N, B = O and C = P . . . but also, N = A, O = B and P = C. So take whichever letter you're given and substitute the letter above or below it. Get it?

B	U	S	T	E	D
O	H	F	G	R	Q

Secret!

No letter in the English alphabet is used more than the letter "E" . . . and none is used less than "Q."

Word Cipher

Using the code key, decipher the missing words in Isaiah 1:19 and Titus 3:1–2 to see what the Bible says about obedience.

If _____ are _____
    L B H   J V Y Y V A T

and _____,
     B O R Q V R A G

you _____ _____ the _____
     J V Y Y   R N G   O R F G

from the _____.
       Y N A Q

Remind the _____to be subject to rulers and
       C R B C Y R

_____, to be
 N H G U B E V G V R F

_____, to be ready to do
   B O R Q V R A G

whatever is _____, to slander no one, to be
         T B B Q

_____ and considerate, and
    C R N P R N O Y R

to show _____ humility toward all men.
     G E H R

A Perfect Fit

Decode the following words, then place them in the puzzle so they all fit!

JVYYVAT

_____

BORQVRAG

_____

ERJNEQ

_____

ZLFGREL

_____

PBQROHFGRE

_____

ZVPX

_____

ABIN

_____

Under Investigation

What does it mean to be willing?
What does it mean to be obedient?

Code 27:

THE ENEMY

There is an enemy out there who wants to trip you up—and his name is Satan. His main goals are to steal, kill and destroy (John 10:10), and he will try to trick you to get what he wants. What's one of the main ways he does this? By putting deceitful thoughts in your mind. That's why it's important to know the difference between God's voice and the devil's voice.

God came to give you life—and anything He tells you matches up with what the Bible says. The devil wants you to think you're worth nothing and that no one loves you. What he says contradicts the Bible. And he wants you to live in fear.

So the next time the devil comes whispering lies, turn a deaf ear his way. Because you know better. You know the Truth!

Code Key

Bust the Code: Mirror, mirror, on the wall . . . In this code, there is a combination of forward and backward letters. The key to breaking it is to always start by reading only the forward letters . . . until you come to a vertical line in the text. Then start reading only the backward letters. Just remember that the vertical line is like a mirror—and when you see it, you start reading the "flip side" of what you had been reading. Get it?

Note: Some letters like "U" and "T" look the same both forward and backward! When you can't tell which direction a letter faces, you have to figure out the other letters first so you can see what you're missing.

Secret!

Ever wonder why your reflection on the back of a spoon is right-side up, while on the front of the spoon it's upside down? It's because the front of the spoon is concave, meaning it "caves in." That causes the light that creates your reflection to shoot off from the spoon at an angle . . . which creates an upside down image to your eye. The back of the spoon, on the other hand, is convex, or "pushed out," which causes the light that creates your reflection to shoot off at a different angle—one that still appears right-side up to your eye.

Word Cipher

Using the mirror code, decipher the missing words in John 8:44, John 10:10, and Luke 10:19 to find out what Jesus said about your enemy.

...there is no _____ in the _____. When he lies,
　　　　　　　　 MTIRꞀUꓘ|NTOHVA　　　　　 AꓷBꓷ|ꓱꓛOVꓷIꓶ

he _____ his _____ _____.
　 ƧAPꓘƧꟺ|AƧꓘPƧꟻ　　 ꟻNUЯAT|IꓷVꟽꟼꟻ　　 ꟼANGAU|UꟻAꝜꓷꟻ

The _____ _____ only to _____ and kill and
　　 ꓛTꓘHI|ƧꟻGꟻ　　 ꓛЯOꝾ|MꓷꟻGꟻ　　　　ꓛꟻꓶT|ꟻBAꓶ

_____; I have come that they may have life, and have
AꝾPꟻƧ|TЯOY

it to the full.

I have _____ you authority to _____ on
　　 GꟻIVꓘ|GꟻꟻN　　　　　　　　　 TꓛЯꓷA|Mꟼꟻꓶꓛꟻ

_____ and scorpions to overcome, all the
Ƨꟻꟻꓱꓘ|ꓘKꟻꟻƧꓛ

power of the _____ nothing will harm you.
　　 ꟻKꓘN|ꟻMY

Mirrored Image?

Mick and Nova think there's something not quite right about this mirror.
Can you find 11 mistakes in their mirrored reflections and solve the mirror code?

IUTH|ANKT'Z   ONON|NƎ   SU9TRZ|ABИƆCDƎ   MЯIRЯ|RЯORЯR!

_____   _____   _____   _____

Under Investigation

How can you tell the difference between a truth and a lie?
What will you do the next time the devil lies to you?

Code 28:

LIVE BY FAITH

There are two ways to live: By faith or by sight (2 Corinthians 5:7). Kids who live by faith live their lives believing what God says is true above all else. Even if they don't see something they've been praying for, no sweat! They know God will provide exactly what they need. Their faith cannot be shaken.

Kids who live by sight live their lives only believing what they see right in front of their faces. If they read a promise in the Bible, they just shrug their shoulders and think it's nothing more than nice words. But God's promises are true! What He said, He will do. Those who live by faith believe that . . . and that's why they have the most adventurous lives ever. They know some of the best things are just out of sight.

Code Key

B U S T E D

<u>B</u>elieve it or not, <u>S</u>uper Sleuth Investigators Mick and

Nova have <u>s</u>olved many crimes not only <u>t</u>hrough shr<u>e</u>w<u>d</u>

investigation, but also through living by faith!

Bust the Code: The code is already there! To bust this code, rather than reading the sentences, only read the letters or sentences that are underlined. Get it?

Secret!

Newspapers have been around since 1605. There are newspapers all around the world, but none has even come close to the circulation of one Soviet newspaper. It was read regularly by more than 33 million people in 1991.

Word Cipher

Reading only the underlined letters and words, decipher the code, revealing 2 Corinthians 5:7.

Super Sleuths Find "Aliens" in Boy's Basement

Last <u>wee</u>k, Mick Gumshoe and Nova Shrewd, once again, reveal<u>e</u>d they had solved another mystery <u>in</u>vol<u>v</u>ing Rock Johans<u>en</u>, who some people think is a <u>bully</u>, and his <u>f</u>riend Sammy. <u>A</u>pparently, ne<u>ith</u>er boy wa<u>n</u>ted <u>to</u> admi<u>t</u> that some<u>b</u>ody el<u>se</u> had ident<u>ifi</u>ed what they had missed: That the "alien light" in Sammy's basement was nothing more than a ni<u>ght</u>light!

_____

_____

_____

Write Between the Lines

Create your own newspaper story below, then underline certain letters and send a message to a friend . . . or clip an article from a real newspaper and do the same. See if they can break the code without telling them how to solve it!

_____

_____

_____

_____

_____

_____

_____

_____

Under Investigation

What do you have faith for that you cannot see yet?
Why is faith more real than sight?

Code 29:

YOUR GIFTS

God has made you unique and placed talents and abilities within you—special gifts—that only you have (Psalm 139:14). Sure, others may have similar gifts, but only *you* can show your gifts the way you can! God wants you to use your gifts to reach the world with His love. That's why He reminds us to stir up the gifts He's put inside us (2 Timothy 1:6).

He doesn't want your gifts to sit idle. He wants you to look for opportunities to use them and make them stronger than ever. What are your gifts? Drawing? Writing? Building? Math? Encouraging others? Something else? Whatever they are, don't forget you have them. Use them today and give God glory!

Code Key

A 01000001	F 01000110	K 01001011	P 01010000	U 01010101	Z 01011010
B 01000010	G 01000111	L 01001100	Q 01010001	V 01010110	
C 01000011	H 01001000	M 01001101	R 01010010	W 01010111	
D 01000100	I 01001001	N 01001110	S 01010011	X 01011000	
E 01000101	J 01001010	O 01001111	T 01010100	Y 01011001	

Bust the Code: This is a common substitution code—binary numbers. These numbers consist of two parts. The numbers under each letter represent that letter. So, 01000001 = A. Here's the hard part: Numbers comprising words are written without spaces. So you must first separate the numbers from each other. Get it?

01000010010101010101001101010100010001010101000100= BUSTED

Secret!

Binary code is made up of the 0's and 1's that computers use when computing. They stand for which computer "bits" are on (1) or off (0). Eight bits together are called a "byte." To the human eye, they sure look confusing . . . but to a computer, they're the native language!

Word Cipher

Using binary code, decipher the missing words in 2 Timothy 1:6 and Psalm 139:14 to see what the Bible says about your gifts.

...I remind you to _____ into
                   01000110010000010100 1110
                   (FAN)

_____ the
01000110010011000100000101001101 01000101
(FLAME)

_____ of _____,
01000111010010010100011001010100   01000111010011110100 0100
(GIFT)   (GOD)

which is in you.

I _____ you
  01010000010100100100000101001001 0101001101000101
  (PRAISE)

_____
01000010010000110100010101000001 01010101010100110101010101010 0110 1000101
(BECAUSE)

_____ _____ fearfully and wonderfully
01001001 0100000101001101
(I)   (AM)

_____.
01001101010000010100010001000101
(MADE)

Fill-In-the-Binary

Using only 0's and 1's, fill in the puzzle below. The numbers added across should equal the numbers on the right. The numbers added down should equal the numbers at the bottom. And the numbers added diagonally should equal the numbers at each corner.

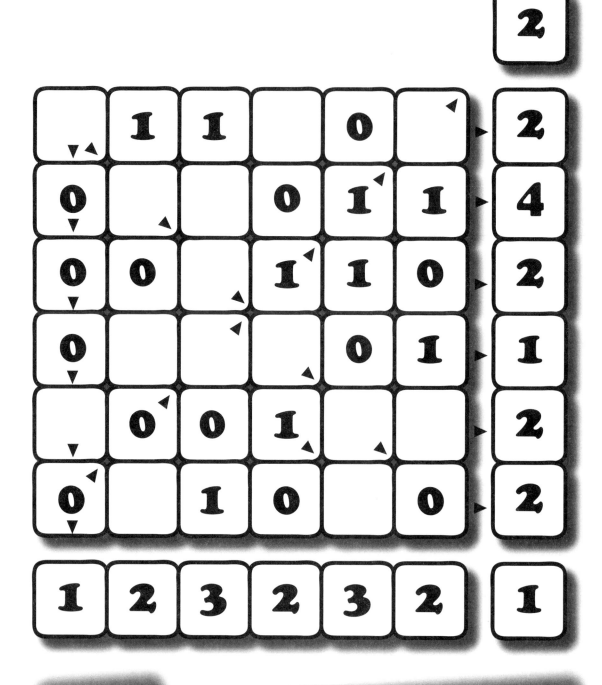

Under Investigation

What is a gift God has put into you?
When was a time you saw your gift in action?

Code 30:

SET AN EXAMPLE

God loves kids like us. While sometimes people think that kids don't have much to offer, God thinks quite differently! He believes we can change the world. He is always ready to move through a young person, if we'll just be committed to Him. The Bible is filled with young people like Samuel and King David, who God used when they were very young.

God goes so far as to believe that we can be examples to others—kids and adults alike—by the things we say, what we believe, and the way we live (1 Timothy 4:12). So get ready . . . God wants to move through you!

Code Key

Oink-oink!

Bust the Code: This code uses Pig Latin! To write in Pig Latin, you have to follow two rules:

1. For words beginning with consonants, move the first consonant sound to the end of the word and add "ay." So "cool" becomes "oolcay" and "crime" becomes "ime-cray" and "scratch" becomes "atchscray."

2. For words beginning with vowels or vowel sounds, just add "ay" to the end of the word. So "earth" becomes "earthay" and "hour" becomes "houray" (because the "h" is silent). Get it?

```
BUSTED
USTEDBAY
```

Secret!

Pig Latin has been around for years and is mainly just a fun word game to play. However, some Pig Latin words like "amscray" have become part of our everyday English language, as slang.

Word Cipher

The entire verse of 1 Timothy 4:12 and John 13:15 has been written in Pig Latin below. Can you decipher them?

Ontday etlay anyoneay ooklay ownday onay ouyay ecausebay ouyay areay oungyay,

_____

_____

utbay etsay anay exampleay orfay ethay elieversbay inay eechspay, inay ifelay, inay ovelay,

_____

_____

inay aithfay anday inay uritypay.

_____

_____

Iay haveay etsay ouyay anay exampleay atthay ouyay ouldshay oday asay

_____

_____

Iay haveay oneday orfay ouyay.

_____

_____

Onguetay Isterstway

Translate these sentences from Pig Latin and then see how fast you can say the tongue twisters!

Imtay ethay urtletay oldtay Omtay otway oughtay onguetay
isterstway.

_____

_____

Eshay ellssay easay ellsshay ybay ethay eashoresay.

_____

_____

Omesay unshay unshinesay onay Undaysay.

_____

_____

Aay oisynay oisenay annoysay aay oseynay eighbornay.

_____

_____

Enwhay oesday ethay istwatchwray apstray opshay utshay?

_____

_____

Under Investigation

How are you a good example to others?
What do you hope others see when they look at you?

BONUS: Create Your Own Code Buster's Code Wheel!

In this book, you've discovered several "substitution codes"—codes where you substitute one letter or number for another to decipher a code. Now you can create your own Code Busters Code Wheel for you and your friends! Here's how it works:

1. Photocopy page 77.

2. Cut out each wheel.

3. Place the smaller wheel inside the larger wheel and place a paper fastener in the center to hold the two wheels together.

4. Now, spin the inner wheel around and stop it wherever you want.

5. Look for the "A" on the outer wheel and note which letter or number it matches up with on the inner wheel. For instance, "A" might match up with "Q". So, "A" = "Q". Hold the wheel in this spot, noting how the other letters line up. This is your code key.

6. Now write a code, substituting the letters you write (from the outer wheel) with the letters that match up on the inner wheel.

7. Give your code to a friend and let them know that "A" = "Q".

8. Now they can spin the wheel so "A" = "Q" and break your code!

For added fun, flip the inside wheel over and write a symbol in place of each letter and number. Now you've got your own symbol-based substitution code, too!

Code Wheel Patterns

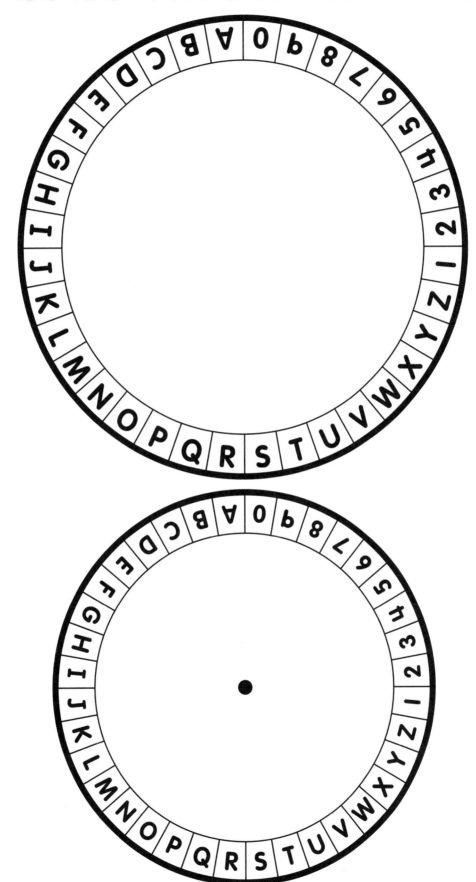

Solutions

Page 6

... my word ... will not return to me empty, but will accomplish what I desire and achieve the purpose for which I sent it. (Isaiah 55:11)

The Lord is faithful and will keep all of his promises. (Psalm 145:13 NIrV)

Page 7
Search-In-Code:

M	I	C	K	G	A	B
E	T	F	N	O	V	A
G	R	R	I	D	J	B
K	U	L	C	Q	O	I
S	E	A	R	C	H	B
P	R	M	O	O	E	L
P	R	O	M	I	S	E

Page 9

It is that he loved us and sent his Son to give his life to pay for our sins. (1 John 4:10 NIrV)
Joke-In-Code: "I once saw a girl eating lobster!"

Page 11

Starting a quarrel is like breaching a dam; so drop the matter before a dispute breaks out.
(Proverbs 17:14)
Superlong Math Code: Problems!

Page 13

Everyone who calls on the name of the Lord will be saved. (Romans 10:13)
Opposites: Hot-cold, wet-dry, up-down, tall-short, first-last

Page 15

Your word is a lamp to my feet and a light for my path. (Psalm 119:105)
Joke-in-Code: It's obviously a mouse on vacation!

Page 17

"Blessed are you when people insult you ... be glad, because great is your reward in heaven. . . ."
(Matthew 5:11–12)
Funny Facts: 1) Some penguins can swim 22 miles per hour. 2) The average person blinks 25 times per minute.

Page 19

My sheep listen to my voice; I know them, and they follow me. (John 10:27)
The voice of the Lord is powerful; the voice of the Lord is majestic. (Psalm 29:4)

Page 21

"Man looks at the outward appearance, but the Lord looks at the heart." (1 Samuel 16:7)
Name Cluster: Answers will vary.

Page 23

For he will command his angels concerning you to guard you in all your ways. (Psalm 91:11)
Graph It: Answers will vary.

Page 25

A cheerful heart is good medicine. . . . (Proverbs 17:22)
Knock-Knock: Olive! Olive who? Olive to solve codes!

Page 27

What is impossible with men is possible with God. (Luke 18:27).
Re: Draw:

1	He is ...		
2	@@@@@		8
3	@ -- @@@		8
4	@| @@@@@		8
5	@| @@@@@		8
6	@ -- @@@		8

Page 29

"Be strong and courageous ... for the Lord your God will be with you wherever you go." (Joshua 1:9)
Square Teaser: There are 20 squares. (12 small squares; squares made from 1, 2, 4, 5; 2, 3, 5, 6; 4, 5, 7, 8; 5, 6, 8, 9; 7, 8, *, 0; 8, 9, 0, #; 1, 2, 3, 4, 5, 6, 7, 8, 9; and 4, 5, 6, 7, 8, 9, *, 0, #.

Page 31

"But as for me and my household, we will serve the Lord." (Joshua 24:15)
Joke-In-Code: It's written with invisible oink!

Page 33

A righteous man may have many troubles, but the Lord delivers him from them all. (Psalm 34:19)
Big Trouble:
BDFHJLNPRTVXZBDFHJLNPRTVXZ (The pattern is every other letter, starting with B!)

Page 35
My God will meet all your needs according to his glorious riches in Christ Jesus. (Philippians 4:19)
Maze Run:

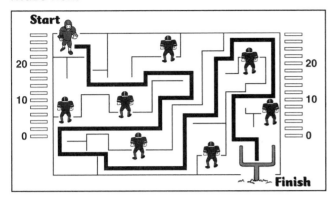

Secret Code: You have made a TOUCHDOWN.

Page 37
. . . the day of the Lord will come like a thief in the night. (1 Thessalonians 5:2)
Completely Shredded: "I think I need to borrow some tape . . . lots of tape!"

Page 39
For the eyes of the Lord range throughout the earth to strengthen those whose hearts are fully committed to him. (2 Chronicles 16:9)
Your Turn!: Answers may vary.

Page 41
If anyone is in Christ, he is a new creation; the old has gone, the new has come! (2 Corinthians 5:17)
Word-in-Words: Possible answers: tea, tear, net, ton, in, on, rot, cat, rat, eat, tin, near, train, rain, cane, toe, tore, are, car, tie, ear, can, ran, at

Page 43
Jesus Christ is the same yesterday and today and forever. (Hebrews 13:8)
That's a Match: Change

Page 45
. . . stand your ground, and after you have done everything . . . to stand. Stand firm. . . .
(Ephesians 6:13–14)

Page 47
Sing joyfully to the Lord, you righteous; it is fitting for the upright to praise him. (Psalm 33:1)
I will praise the Lord all my life; I will sing praise to my God as long as I live. (Psalm 146:2)

Page 48
Flag Scramble:
1) Love others 2) Shout 3) Sing 4) Pray 5) Give
6) Clap 7) Lift your hands

Page 50
Be kind and compassionate to one another, forgiving each other, just as in Christ God forgave you. (Ephesians 4:32)
Bear with each other and forgive whatever grievances you may have against one another. Forgive as the Lord forgave you. (Colossians 3:13)

Page 51
This super spiral code reveals another scripture verse about forgiveness: Mark 11:25: "When you stand praying, if you hold anything against anyone, forgive him, so that your Father in heaven may forgive you your sins."

Page 53
But seek first his kingdom and his righteousness, and all these things will be given to you as well. (Matthew 6:33)

Page 54
Capture the Flag:

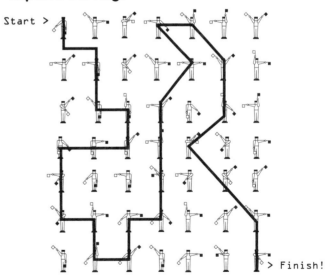

Page 56
. . . let your light shine before men, that they may see your good deeds and praise your Father in heaven. (Matthew 5:16)

Page 57
Memory Challenge:

Page 59
And the peace of God, which transcends all understanding, will guard your hearts and your minds in Christ Jesus. (Philippians 4:7)

Page 60
The Right Road:
Car #2 made the green light.
Secret Word: Zoom!

Page 62
If you are willing and obedient, you will eat the best from the land. (Isaiah 1:19)
Remind the people to be subject to rulers and authorities, to be obedient, to be ready to do whatever is good, to slander no one, to be peaceable and considerate, and to show true humility toward all men. (Titus 3:1–2)

Page 63
A Perfect Fit:
Willing, Obedient, Reward, Mystery, Codebuster, Mick, Nova.

Page 65
. . . there is no truth in [the devil]. When he lies, he speaks his native language. (John 8:44)
The thief comes only to steal and kill and destroy; I have come that they may have life, and have it to the full. (John 10:10)
I have given you authority to trample on snakes and scorpions and to overcome all the power of the enemy; nothing will harm you. (Luke 10:19)

Page 66
Mirrored Image?
The following changes appear between the images: Nova's glasses are no longer white. Nova's shirt has a collar. Mick is holding a pencil. Mick's belt is no longer white. The plant lost its leaves. The plant vase doesn't have a heart on it. The table has a tablecloth. The colors switched on the tabletop and table stand. The picture on the wall doesn't have a tree in it. The colors in the picture switched. The picture frame is no longer white.
Mirrored Code: That's One Strange Mirror!

Page 68
We live by faith, not by sight. (2 Corinthians 5:7)

Page 69
Write Between the Lines: Answers will vary.

Page 71
. . . I remind you to fan into flame the gift of God, which is in you. (2 Timothy 1:6)
I praise you because I am fearfully and wonderfully made. (Psalm 139:14)

Page 72
Fill-in-the Binary:

0	1	1	0	0	0
0	1	1	0	1	1
0	0	0	1	1	0
0	0	0	0	0	1
1	0	0	1	0	0
0	0	1	0	1	0

Page 74
Don't let anyone look down on you because you are young, but set an example for the believers in speech, in life, in love, in faith and in purity.
(1 Timothy 4:12)
I have set you an example that you should do as I have done for you. (John 13:15)

Page 75
Onguetay Isterstway
1. Tim the turtle told Tom two tough tongue twisters.
2. She sells sea shells by the seashore.
3. Some shun sunshine on Sunday.
4. A noisy noise annoys a nosey neighbor.
5. When does the wristwatch strap shop shut?